MW01291588

Emotional Intelligence:

*100+ Skills, Tips, Tricks &
Techniques to Improve
Interpersonal Connection,
Control Your Emotions, Build
Self Confidence & Find Long
Lasting Success!*

Kevin Moore © 2016

Disclaimer:

Introduction

First off, I'd like to thank you for purchasing this book. By getting this guide you've shown that you're serious about improving yourself and growing emotionally as a person. Self reflection can be difficult. Learning to understand and deal with your emotions in a healthy way will take time and patience on your part. Hopefully this book will help to clarify things and make that process smoother.

Communication is the cornerstone of our daily lives. Without it we have nothing. The world as we know it would cease to exist and our species would have gone extinct long ago. Take a few moments and think on everything you do each day that hinges on your ability to communicate with those around you. Pretty much everything of importance am I right. Since communication is such an important aspect of our lives, you would think people would put a greater priority on understanding what makes communication possible and how to improve those skills to make their lives better. That's where emotional intelligence and this book come in.

Emotional intelligence, often referred to as EI or EQ, is a major part of who we are as people and how we deal with the situations and people around us. In fact, many believe working on your emotional intelligence is the most important aspect of personal development a person can undertake. So what does emotional intelligence mean? Well, it's defined as "our capacity to control, be aware of, and express our emotions, while handling our interpersonal relationships both empathetically and judiciously. Emotional intelligence also allows us to recognize other people's emotions and how to use that information to guide both our behavior and thinking."

In this book, I'll be discussing emotional intelligence, the role it plays in our everyday lives, and how you can take what you've learned to become more confident, control your emotional state, and improve your relationships, both professionally and privately. I'll also be going over some tips and tricks I've picked up over the years, along with a resource guide that I think you'll find useful.

I'm excited to get started. Let's begin!

Chapter One: An Introduction to Emotional Intelligence

What is Emotional Intelligence?

As I touched upon in the introduction, emotional intelligence is a key factor in how we connect to the people around us. When it comes to our success and happiness in relationships, personal and career goals, our EQ or emotional intelligence often means more than our actual IQ or intellectual ability. Emotional intelligence allows us to turn our intention into future action, it also allows us to make well informed decisions on the things that are most important to us. EQ allows us to better connect to the people around us in nurturing and productive ways.

By being able to identify, understand, use, and manage our emotions in a positive way, we are able to communicate more effectively, relieve stress, overcome more challenges, empathize with those around us, and defuse potential conflicts. EQ allows us to understand and recognize what the people around us are emotionally experiencing. This process is mainly a nonverbal one that influences how we connect with people and informs our thinking on how to handle certain situations.

Intellectual ability and emotional intelligence differ greatly from one another. IQ is something we're born with, while EQ is something we learn over time. Improving emotional intelligence can be done at any stage of life and is something that is possible for everyone to do, regardless of intellect. It's not enough to simply learn about EQ, in order for it to mean something, you must be willing to apply it to your daily life. This process can be difficult at times. Changing a behavior permanently requires a willingness to work on how you deal with stress while learning how to remain aware emotionally. Trust me when I say the hard work is worth it. The sooner you're in control of your own life, the sooner you'll be able to work towards achieving the life you've always dreamed of.

The Four Attributes of Emotional Intelligence

Emotional intelligence is normally defined around these four attributes. These four attributes all work in tandem to give you the ability to handle any situations that come your way.

1. *Self Awareness* – The ability to recognize emotion in yourself and see how these emotions affect both your behavior and thoughts. Being self aware means you know where your strengths and weaknesses are. It also means having self confidence.

2. *Self-management* – The ability to control impulsive urges, behaviors, and feelings. Being able to manage yourself means you can deal with your emotions in a productive and healthy fashion, adapt to new and unforeseen circumstances, and follow through on promises and commitments.

3. *Social awareness*_ – The ability to understand the needs, concerns and emotions of those around you. Being socially aware means you must feel comfortable when your in social situations, can pick up on the emotional cues of those around you, and recognize the dynamics of the organizations or groups you're a part of.

4. *Relationship management* – The ability to maintain and develop strong healthy relationships, influence and inspire those around you, communicate in a clear fashion, manage conflicts, and work well with others in a team setting.

The Importance Of Emotional Intelligence

Why is emotional intelligence so important? As you may already know it's not always the smartest people who have the most fulfilled or successful lives. I can think of quite a few examples in my own group of friends who are brilliant in the classroom but completely inept when face to face with other people and have problems holding down a job for more than a few months at a time. Having a high IQ isn't always enough to allow you to lead the life you want to lead.

Sure, having a high IQ will open up certain doors, like better colleges to choose from, but it's your EQ that will allow you to thrive wherever you eventually end up, by allowing you to deal with the emotions and stress you'll face on a daily basis. I find that the people who get the most out of life have their EQ and IQ working together in tandem. Continual self improvement and reflection will allow one to elevate their status and gradually build a better life.

To get ahead in life you need to hone your emotions to the situation at hand. For example, holding on to grudges with an employer who can either help or break your career. A person with low emotional intelligence will let those past feelings cloud their judgment and make their disdain known to anyone who will listen. This will normally result in being fired or overlooked for future promotions. A person with a high level of emotional intelligence will recognize that holding this grudge will only harm them in the long run and let go of it. Now this is not to say you need to like this employer, but you do need to show them respect in the workplace in order to ensure that when it comes time to ask for a raise or promotion you're in a position to get what you're looking for. This is just one small example of how emotional intelligence plays a crucial role in your life.

Now while this example is a little extreme let me assure you that everyone can benefit from improving their emotional intelligence. Maybe you're very socially aware and have great people skills but lack the ability to manage your own life and relationships. Perhaps, you're great at managing your own emotions but have difficulty in social settings. Once you're able to diagnosis your own areas of weakness you'll be able to work on them and improve your life.

The Five Areas Emotional Intelligence Can Make a Difference In

Once you understand the different attributes of emotional intelligence it's important to understand what parts of your life emotional intelligence can have a direct impact on.

1. Mental Wellness - How we behave and view the world is greatly impacted by our emotional intelligence. Having a high level of emotional intelligence has been found to directly correlate to increased self confidence and reduced anxiety.

2. *Physical Health* - Emotional intelligence is crucial to our ability to properly care for our body and reduce stress. Dealing with our emotions in a healthy way has a tremendous effect on our overall well being.

3. *Conflict Resolution* - When we learn the ability to recognize other people's emotions and feel empathy it becomes easier to solve arguments and disagreements. This also allows us to handle problems easier than those without this ability as we can better understand the needs of others.

4. *Relationships* - When you understand your own feelings you're better able to convey those feelings to the people around you. When you have a high level of emotional intelligence you're more aware of how the people around you feel. This leads you to naturally treat those around you in a way that you'd wish to be treated yourself.

5. *Prosperity & Success* - People with a high EQ are more confident and therefore more willing to go after the things they want out of life. These type of people will spend less time procrastinating and will have the inner strength needed to concentrate on and eventually achieve their goals. High EQ helps you understand that postponing small immediate satisfaction is worth it for longer lasting success down the road.

Tools for Improving our Emotional Intelligence

Here a few of tools anyone can use to help improve their level of emotional intelligence.

1. *Meditation* - In order to become emotionally intelligent you'll first need to learn how to manage and control your emotional state. Doing this is harder than it sounds. Our bodies want to naturally react in a certain manner when dealing with certain emotions. To counteract those tendencies we must train our mind and body to think before reacting and evaluate what we're feeling and why we're feeling it. Meditation is a great way to to do this. By meditating daily we can train ourselves to remain calm and self detached under even the most stressful situations. Getting good at meditation takes time and practice. Keep at it and I promise you'll start thinking clearer and feeling more positive, while having more control over your emotional state. There are many forms of meditation you can try. I suggest checking out a few and sticking with the one that best fits into your daily lifestyle. Everyone has their own preferences when it comes to how they meditate. The important part is that you get started.

2. *Mindfulness* - This one goes hand in hand with meditation. It's about being aware of each moment and everything around you. By practicing mindfulness on a daily basis you'll naturally become more self aware and better able to manage your emotions and difficult relationships. I also found it improved my focus and concentration immensely.

3. *Affirmations* - I love affirmations. They empower and motivate me whenever I need a pick me up. I have a list that I keep handy on my phone that I can reference whenever I feel the need. When I'm feeling down or negative about something I pull out my list and repeat a few affirmations out loud to achieve a more positive mindset. Daily affirmations are a big part of my morning routine. This is one of my favorite tools.

4. *Emotional Freedom Technique (EFT)* -   This technique is one that borrows from Chinese acupuncture. It involves tapping certain parts of your body when you're feeling overwhelmed with an emotion. These emotions can range from anger, to sadness, to fear, to frustration. Whenever you feel an emotion overpowering you, begin tapping with your first two fingers on one of the following body parts. These parts include your outer hand, rib cage, right below your eyes, or on your chin. Continue tapping this area for a few minutes while focusing on the emotion. Continue to do this until the emotion subsides. Personally, I've only used this one a few times when I was first starting out. I prefer practicing mindfulness and meditation. I did find it valuable when I was in a public situation and felt overwhelmed. I just did the tapping discreetly on my outer hand so no one would see me and wonder what was going on.

Chapter Two: Self Perception, Mindfulness & Emotional Intelligence

Learning to understand yourself is a key component to emotional intelligence. Having a healthy perception of yourself will allow you to confidently move towards building strong relationships, managing stress, and achieving the goals you set for yourself both personally and professionally. Self perception is the prism with which you view yourself in. Most people don't take the time to understand themselves as well as they should. When they experience emotional outbursts they don't reflect on what was causing them to feel that particular set of emotions and how those feelings were impacting other areas of their life. In this section, I'm going to discuss the importance of self perception and how to discover who we are and how to get to who we want to be.

If you're not able to be self aware you'll never be able to be aware of those around you. Learning to become more self aware is the first step in raising your emotional intelligence. To get started I suggest documenting how you feel on a daily basis. Take notes a few times each day on how you're feeling and examine what happened to make you feel that way. By recording this you'll be able to go back over your notes and start to see what types of patterns have developed. This will allow you to understand types of people or situations that trigger certain emotions in you. Having this information will allow you to examine yourself more closely and figure out ways to better manage your emotions and hone them to benefit you instead of holding you back.

Self perception is often broken down into three smaller categories. Once you've learned how to get the most out of each of these areas in your life you'll be well on your way to a happier more stable life. I'm going to briefly discuss each of these sections below.

1. *Self Regard* - You need to put yourself first. However, you need to to this without being arrogant or insecure. You need to understand your strengths and put them to use in ways that will benefit you. If you don't respect yourself you'll have a hard time respecting other people. I suggest getting some honest feedback from people you trust who care about you and know you. The goal is to take action based on what you learned about yourself.

2. *Self Awareness* - When you have self awareness you're able to manage how your emotions will impact those around you and you're also able to read other people's emotional non verbal cues. The more aware you are the better you'll be able to have and keep meaningful relationships in your life. As practice try reading the facial expressions of the people you come in contact with on a daily basis. These cues are things like frowning, smiling, pursed lips, and furrowed brows. You'll also want to observe people's body language when there in an emotional situation and see how they respond bothy physically and verbally. It's easiest to do this when you're not an active participant in the emotional exchange. After the situation is over think over the scene in your head and imagine how you could handle it better if it was you. Doing this exercise is good practice for when you do get in an emotional confrontation with someone.

3. *Self Actualization* - This component has to do with becoming more purpose driven. This can be for something in your personal life or professional life. Seeking meaning in what your doing and how you want to live takes some courage. It requires you step up and make the commitments necessary to gain what you desire. A good way to further develop this muscle is by leveraging your skills, strengths, and talent. Take some time to figure out what those are for you and then go about finding ways to use those things to improve your life and get the things you want out of it.

One of the best ways to train our minds in the art of self perception is mindfulness. What is that you ask? Well, mindfulness is the art of training your mind to be aware at every given moment. Being mindful allows you to step back from a situation and figure out how you feel before responding. It allows you to see what is happening around you because your paying attention to both yourself and the world. Mindfulness is all about experiencing life instead of just watching it happen around you.

How to Get Started On The Path to Mindfulness

So you've decided you want to become more mindful. However, you're not quite sure how to go about achieving this. Well, in this section I'll go over some of the different steps you can take in order to start down the path to leading a life of mindfulness.

There are several different practices and disciplines that help to cultivate mindfulness. A few of these include tai chi, yoga, qigong and meditation. All of these are wonderful methods. Most of my personal experience lies in mindfulness meditation.

There are two main forms of meditation along with various other types that focus on certain areas we want to work on. I'll briefly go over both main forms and the various types so that you understand the differences between them.

Two Main Forms of Meditation

1. Concentration Meditation – This type of meditation is where you narrow your attention and focus on your breath along with an object, image, or sound. You do this in order to help calm your mind and allow for more clarity and a higher awareness to emerge.

2. Mindful Meditation – This type of meditation is where you open up your awareness and attention to all sensations, thoughts, feelings, sounds, smells and images without judgment or evaluation.

Various Meditation Types

1. Awareness Meditation – This is the practice of moment to moment observation of your surroundings, and the world, as they truly happen to be. This type of meditation promotes a stable, clear awareness of one's thoughts without any judgment.

2. Loving Kindness Meditation – This kind of meditation is a heartfelt wish of happiness and well being to not only yourself, but extending out to everyone else around you. This meditation helps to reinforce our emotions of compassion, kindness, love and appreciation.

3. Japa Meditation – This type of meditation is a repetition of a Sanskrit term or mantra while using the rotation of a rosary or beaded Mala. This meditation is considered to be extremely effective for tension and stress.

4. Transcendental Meditation TM – This kind of meditation has been widely researched and uses a practiced seven step program that gives each of its students a personal mantra or sound, using a comfortable seated technique with eyes closed.

5. Passage Meditation – This type of meditation uses inspirational and spiritual passages, that are supported by seven different disciplines. These disciplines fit any non religious or religious philosophy, enabling a practitioner to stay kind, calm, and focused.

6. Vipassana Meditation or Insight Meditation – This kind of meditation practices mindfulness and shedding a light on the subtlest workings of our mind. This is done in order to bring the true nature of our reality into sharper focus. This allows us to have a much deeper interconnection between our body and mind.

7. Yoga – The benefits of practicing yoga are both clear and very conclusive. This type of movement meditation, using relaxation techniques and breathing, allows you to drastically reduce stress and tension, from both your mind and body.

8. Qigong & Tai Chi - These art forms speak to people who enjoy martial arts and want to learn meditation and relaxation techniques. These techniques are very popular among seniors.

I'm also a big fan of walking meditation. I find it's something I can easily weave into my daily life. I keep my walks simple, however, some people prefer elaborate labyrinth walking or even trying their hand at meditative dance. I've yet to do either so I can't comment on how effective they are in relation to just a normal walking meditation.

Simple Meditation Techniques For Beginners

Most traditional forms of meditation come from some type of older religious origins. However, you don't need to be a monk in order to reap the rewards meditation provides.

What form of meditation you decide is best for you, will depend on your purpose and preference. For instance, I stick to mindful meditation, walking meditations, and yoga. I found those are what work best for me in my life.

In this section, I'm going to discuss simple ways you can begin opening your mind to meditation. The purpose of these suggestions are to start learning how to begin slowing down and calming your mind.

Breath Awareness Meditation

This is a very effective form of meditation all by itself. Let's go over how you can begin to start practicing this form of meditation.

First, try sitting upright in a relaxed position, keeping your spine straight. Begin by closing your eyes. Take a few moments to yourself and simply be. Notice whatever you happen to be experiencing, in that particular moment, without taking any action on it.

Once you've allowed yourself to get settled in, start noticing your breath as it both leaves and enters your body. Don't try and manipulate your breathing patterns in any way. Experience your breathing and feel how the air moves in and out of your nose along with how your body moves when breathing.

At times your mind will begin to wander away from your breath. That's completely normal, it doesn't matter. It's actually a part of this meditation! If you notice, you're no longer only observing your breath, you can easily focus your attention back to it when your mind wanders.

Let each of your experiences, emotions, thoughts, and bodily sensations continuously come and go, while staying in the background of your awareness of your breath. Notice how these things all come and go, effortlessly and automatically, like your breath.

Over time, you'll learn the different tendencies your mind has. You'll see how it tries to hold onto certain experiences, while resisting others. Letting your mind settle down naturally will allow you to recognize these tendencies, while giving you the opportunity to let go of them and any of the negativity attached to them.

Audio Or Guided Meditation

It's also possible to find a serene and calm peace of mind while doing mundane activities. Things that you find to be boring or routine can be changed into mindfulness exercises you can use for deeper self relaxation.

For example, I enjoy walking so I turned the time I used on my walks into time I can practice walking meditation. You can meditate while doing a variety activities. Anything from sports like biking and swimming to hobbies like painting and gardening.

Another simple way to begin meditating is by seeking out relaxing activities when you begin to feel stressed. Listening to some music, writing in a journal, and reading are all good examples. These activities all work in a similar way. They help to focus your mind while also lowering your beta brain activity. This helps to naturally put your mind in a more meditative state.

Guided relaxation meditations are great form of meditation that uses instruction, imagery, stories, natural sound effects and music to help you focus, relax and follow along. You can find these offered in every format imaginable from CD's and DVD to MP3 downloads and cassette tapes.

Another popular form of meditation is Brain Wave Entrainment. These audio CD programs have been gaining in popularity. This form of meditation uses binaural beats to help synchronize your brain waves and then alter the brain wave frequencies into a specific state of consciousness. What this does is enable a person to reach a deeper state of meditation very quickly.

The different forms and methods of meditation are almost endless. You're really only limited by your imagination. The sooner you get started, the sooner you'll start to enjoy the simple pleasure of existing and raising your level of emotional intelligence.

Chapter Three: Developing Emotional Intelligence In The Workplace

Developing Emotional Intelligence In the Workplace

Studies have shown that people with higher levels of emotional intelligence are more successful in the workplace. The reason for this is because these people have highly developed interpersonal skills that allow them to motivate, inspire, and relate to their fellow coworkers. Emotional intelligence allows a person to diffuse arguments between workers while reducing stress and tension among those around them. These types of skills will allow you to climb the ladder quickly and show that you have the ability to effectively manage a set of people in a business environment.

Every business needs to address how well the people that are part of the business work with one another. Emotional intelligence at work is all about relationships and how they function. These relationships include worker to worker, management to management, management to worker and employees to customers and vendors. If there are rifts or issues in any of these areas you're business won't be as successful as it could be. It's also important to see any issues that begin to form in advance before they become bigger problems down the road. Many companies fail each day because the people who work there don't have the interpersonal skills to keep the business moving forward and running smoothly.

Businesses that are emotionally intelligent have staff who remain aligned with your business ideals, are committed to the business succeeding, productive, motivated, efficient, happy, confident, and likable. Remember, emotional intelligence can be applied to every type of person to person interaction that occurs in the business. From customer service to keeping staff motivated and willing to work, emotional intelligence plays a vital part in the day to day success of any business.

So that brings the question, how can we develop emotional intelligence in the workplace? Let's look at it from the both the employers and employees perspectives.

From the employees perspective, employees are looking for jobs that they're passionate about and that take advantage of their talents. Employees want their employers to be mindful of who they are and what they need. Employees today aren't like our parents who mainly viewed jobs as a paycheck. They want a career they can be excited about and grow with. If an employee doesn't feel their employers cares about these things they'll be less engaged and less productive.

From the employers perspective, management can be more effective when they provide an environment that fosters, employee engagement, productivity, and teamwork. If an employer is too focused on their personal gain and not the needs of their staff they'll suffer in the long run. Employers should have a management team filled with capable mentors who are committed to helping the other employees navigate the workplace and become better versions of themselves. Management needs to realize that everyone is different and therefore needs to be handled in a way that gets the most out of them. That is why emotional intelligence is so important. Being able to recognize who needs what and when is an amazing skill to have at one's disposal.

When it comes right down to it business leaders need to be emotionally intelligent in order to be more efficient and effective at achieving desired results and maximizing all outcomes. Employees need to be more emotionally intelligent in order to work their way up the ladder and achieve the job and success they desire.

Here are five different ways employers can lead using emotional intelligence to help boost employees productivity.

1. *Show That You Care About The People Around You.*

Caring about others is a simple thing you can do. However, it needs to feel genuine in both tone and delivery. Management should always remember to balance what their mind says with what their heart says. In work terms this means you can't always be intense and overbearing about what you require out of your employees. Intensity works but only when used in the right way to keep or build momentum on a project. By being more compassionate and caring you'll show your workers that the job their doing for you is being appreciated. Employees don't want to feel like a cog in the machine. They want to feel valued and appreciated. You don't need to babysit them or hold their hand, just let them know when they've done a good job and remind them of what things are expected from their job performance. If you do this properly, people will perform at a higher level.

2. *Help Your Employees Feel Significant*

Management should always try to be motivating their employees by showing them how their job benefits not only the company but their personal life as well. In today's society, employees want to feel like their making an impact, that their leaving their mark. Give them ways that allow them to feel this way and they'll produce much more. When an employee gets a taste of success they'll being willing to work harder to maintain it or surpass it.

3. *Embrace People's Differences In Order to Generate a Big Difference.*

In today's world people's differences are very apparent. People like to feel authentic and will appreciate an employer who embraces those differences. By being sensitive on how you leverage and manage your employees differences you can assemble an excellent team that has people with unique talents, abilities and world views working together towards a unified goal. When conflict arises within a team, look for any common ground between the people to help you in resolving the dispute. By viewing differences as opportunities you're putting your company in a better position to succeed. The more you include people that are different the more the opportunities around you will grow.

4. Be As Accountable As Your Employees.

Although management is in charge it doesn't have to mean their not viewed as equals with their employees. This means as management you need to hold yourself just as accountable as a regular employee, enforcing the same rules on yourself that you'd expect your employees to follow. Employees appreciate it when their leaders are open and available. They want to feel like an integral part of the team. They don't want to view it as management versus employee.

If management does something that is wrong they should be transparent about it and admit the mistake. Employees want to see that their leadership can be trusted. Doing so will make you more genuine and real in their eyes. Employees will support and follow management that is easy to approach and easy to relate to. They want management that will get in the trenches when necessary and fight alongside them. Management being accountable defines their real intentions. The more you are accountable, the more your employees will end up trusting you.

5. Always Be Mindful Of Your Employees Needs.

If you notice that your employees are not reaching their potential, or that productivity has decreased, you're doing something wrong as their leader. You need to be sensitive of your employees needs and realize when there are issues that need to be addressed. Everyone can increase and improve their levels of productivity and performance. These improvements will only come with continuous feedback, suggestions, and recommendations on your part. If you're not holding up your end as management how can you expect the employees to hold up theirs.

A team is always more powerful than it's individual parts, however, you need to constantly be guiding your team for it to sustain and improve it's level of performance. Get the most out of your employees by becoming mindful of any needs they have. Figure out what each individual employee needs to continue maturing and growing in their assigned job.

Employee Assessments

You may also want to try and get your staff professionally evaluated. The ESCI (Emotionally and Social Competency Inventory), is the only assessment and development tool worked on by the leading authority of emotional intelligence Daniel Goleman. This study offers a 360 degree view of your employees and is more effective than normal emotional intelligence tests that can be skewed by the user. If you want to assess your team properly than this might be the way to go.

Here is a link where you can check it out and see if it's right for your company:

http://www.haygroup.com/leadershipandtalentondemand/ourproducts/topsellers.aspx

Another solution is hiring people with high EQ to begin with. Doing this will set you up for success from the outset. Many people feel this is the better approach than trying to improve the emotional intelligence of your current staff, however, I've seen both methods be effective when used correctly. Some employees will thrive when you help them develop a higher level of EQ, while others will resist change and may need to be let go of in favor of someone who has the qualities you're looking for. I think the best approach is a healthy mixture of bringing in new people with the proper motivation, mindset and desire while still trying to develop your current employees EQ.

Whichever way you choose to get there is up to you and your business. In the end, what matters is that you have an emotionally intelligent group of people working for you that will achieve a maximum level of effectiveness and put you and your company in the best position for long term success.

Chapter Four: Developing Emotional Intelligence & Interpersonal Skills In Social Interactions

When talking about emotional intelligence the term "social skills" is made in reference to the types of skills one needs to influence and handle other people's emotions in an effective manner. To some this might seem like a type of manipulation but it's not. Instead, it's simply understanding our own and other people's body language. For example, I now that when I smile at someone their naturally going to smile back, which in turns makes them feel more positive. There are times when this doesn't work or have the intended effect but I've found it to hold true in general.

In this section I'm going to discuss some of the different social skills and how they relate to our emotional intelligence. The goal of this chapter is to give you and understanding of the skills you'll want to improve on in order to raise your own EQ level.

Persuasion and Influencing

You'll often run into situations where you'll need to convince, persuade or influence someone to do something that you want them to do. Now these can be for major things or minor things, from getting your kid to clean their room to getting someone to do something against their better judgment. What it's for doesn't really make a difference. The main point is that the art of persuasion and influence is something that you'll want to learn to get good at. These skills can be improved and learned just like any other skill. Granted, for some people it might come a little more naturally than others but even if you're someone who struggles with this you can improve over time with practice.

Two forms of persuasion that aren't effective long term:

1. *Coercion* - This involves falling back on your authority to get other people to do what you want. For example, this can be a parent telling their kid to do their chores or their grounded. I find this method of persuasion to be the least effective as the person involved is forced to do something instead of wanting to do it. This tactic can also breed contempt and hurt feelings if done too often or in a cruel way.

2. *Nagging* - Some people try to persuade others by constantly talking and badgering the people around them until they get what they want. This is can be effective but more often it's just annoying. For example a spouse nagging their significant other until they finish the chores. Again, not a fan of this method.

How to persuade successfully:

In order to be good at persuasion, research has shown that it requires a a few different components. Each of these components rely heavily on emotion and how you interact with others using your communication skills. For instance, people are more easily persuaded by people they feel are reliable, trustworthy, sincere, entertaining, organized, responsible, and keep the promises they make.

People with good persuasion skills are often found to have high levels of self esteem and confidence. They believe the things they are saying and other people sense that belief. Another key component is empathy and listening skills. When you listen you're able to learn what people feel and it will allow you to build rapport with them. You're much more likely to get influenced by your friend than by a stranger. Building a bond with someone brings down their guard and allows you to subtly push your position without having to be overbearing about it. Remember, the easiest way to get someone else to do something is to make them think it was their idea in the first place and to get them to want the same things that you want.

The more you raise your EQ level and practice your communication skills the better you'll get at influencing and persuading others. Personally, my improvement was natural. Over the course of time I began to notice I was having a much easier time getting people to do the things I was asking of them and I began hearing the word "YES" a lot more often. I didn't set out to learn the art of persuasion but that skill set evolved as I worked on my social interactions.

Building Rapport

Being able to build understanding with the people around you will make communicating much easier. Building rapport can happen naturally, some people just get along well from the outset, this is often how strong friendships are forged. On the flip side, you can build rapport with someone by finding some common interests and shared experiences. By actively listening and being empathetic you can develop a bond with almost anyone.

Learning to build rapport is an important tool to have at your disposal. Emotionally intelligent people are able to connect with the people around them by utilizing this skill. It's important in all forms of social interaction from work to personal life. Being able to get along with people will take you farther in life than if you're distant and unavailable.

Relationships are easier to have and maintain when you've developed a sense of understanding between both parties. For some people it can be stressful to meet and engage with new people. Low EQ people will often have awkward body language and a difficult time starting or holding a conversation. If you fall into this boat don't worry there are steps you can follow to get better in these exchanges. Try to stay calm and relax. The more you practice building rapport with people the better you'll become at it.

Here are the two steps you can take to help build rapport:

1. *Breaking The Ice*

This step is for when you first meet a new person. You want to start off by reducing any tension so that both parties can feel more relaxed and better able to communicate. You should begin by using non threatening topics as small talk. These can include weather, sports, travel, or friends in common. Try and find some shared experiences you both have but avoid talking too much about yourself or asking the other party direct questions. The key is to keep things light and polite.

Once you've done that it's time to try and inject some humor into the situation. Laughing together will help to create a sense of harmony. Tell an inoffensive joke about yourself or a funny story or circumstance you were involved in. Do not make fun of other people. This will have the opposite effect and could make the other party feel more defensive.

Be aware of your mannerisms and body language. You want to keep eye contact for at least 55% of the time. People need to feel that you're interested and paying attention. When they talk lean slightly inward. It will help to further indicate your listening.

Be inclusive. Don't ignore the other party if you're in a group of people. You also don't want to focus only on them and make them feel like their being interrogated. Try to let the conversation take its natural course. This one can take some practice to find the right balance but with some work you'll get the hang of it.

The last one is be empathetic. Let the other party know that you're able to see both sides of an issue, and that their opinion is valued. Your goal is to find similarities you share with one another and build a rapport using them.

2. Non Verbal Rapport

After you've had an initial conversation and broken the ice it's important to stay focused and relaxed. At this point non verbal communication will play a large role in rapport building. The way we maintain and build rapport after we break the ice is through subconsciously matching non verbal cues, our eye contact, body language, tone of voice, and facial expressions. People are naturally inclined to do this step in order to avoid conflict so don't fight it. Remember to pay attention to your body language and be more aware of the how you're interacting with the other party. Put some effort into making sure you don't come off poorly. Controlling non verbal cues took me a while to learn and feel comfortable with but after a while it became second nature. The more emotionally intelligent you become the more natural it will feel.

On the other side of things you want to learn how the other party is feeling so you can adjust accordingly. Reading another person's body language can help you avoid getting off track or offending the other party. Remember, you want to keep them interested and engaged in the conversation without making them feel threatened or attacked.

Some questions to ask yourself:

Am I sounding arrogant or rude?

Am I maintaining a good amount of eye contact?

Am I crossing my legs or arms?

Am I being empathetic?

What is their body language indicating?

Am I talking too much and being overbearing?

Now that you've worked on both steps it's time to put these skills to good use. You want to be on your best behavior when trying to build rapport with someone. You'll often hear the saying "Put your best foot forward." That saying can applied to this scenario. When you're trying to build rapport you want someone to not only like you but feel comfortable in your presence. You want them to trust you.

Some things you'll want to do when rapport building besides the above questions include paying compliments, listening without judgment, be honest even if you don't have an answer to a question, be funny but not offensive, and be genuine. By doing those things you'll put yourself in a great position to form a deeper understanding and rapport with just about anyone.

Communication Skills

Communicating effectively is the #1 life skill you'll need to get the most of out of your life. The world revolves around our ability to communicate with one another. Developing this skill will help every aspect of your life, from social to professional. It's never too late to begin. By definition communication is "the act of exchanging information from one spot to another, either by voice, written word, non verbal cues, or visual aid." How good a job we do at transmitting and receiving this information is a measure of our skill in communicating.

In this section, I'm going to discuss a few of the different skills that one will want to master when trying to improve their communication skills. People with high EQ are deft at not only expressing their own feelings but recognizing how those around them feel. It's important to master each of the below skills as they will all work together to allow you to communicate more effectively on a whole.

<u>Here are two important communication skills to focus on:</u>

1. Listening Skills

Being able to actively listen is an important communication skill. People spend on average 45% of their time listening to others. Many people take this skill for granted. Listening isn't the same as simply hearing something. Listening is so important I would rank it as the number one communication skill to master. Without the ability to properly listen, messages can easily get misinterpreted leading to a communication breakdown which in turn leads to frustration and negative feelings. Many of the most powerful and successful people in the world say they owe their success to their ability to listen.

Listening can be broken down into ten principles. I've included a list of these principles down below. They should help guide you on how to become a better listener. Once you've learned how to follow all these steps you'll have mastered the art of listening.

1. Stop Talking - When another person is talking shut up and let them speak. Don't talk over them or interrupt them.

2. Relax - Focus only on the person speaking. Shut off your mind to outside noise. Try only concentrating on the messages the speaker is trying to communicate to you.

3. Make The Speaker Feel At Ease - Concentrate, focus and use body language or encouraging words to let them know you'd like them to continue. You also want to keep good eye contact without staring the person down.

4. Avoid External Distractions - Don't engage in other activities while listening. Don't shuffle your papers or play with your phone. This type of behavior will make you come off as disinterested or bored and will disrupt the person speaking.

5. Empathize - Try your best to see the other person's point of view. Imagine you were in their shoes. How would you react under the same circumstances.

6. Patience - Let the speaker go at their own pace. Don't jump in the first time they pause for a moment. Give them some time and be sure that they've finished speaking.

7. Avoid Personal Preferences - Just because you view things a certain way doesn't mean other people feel the same way about those things. Don't let yourself get irritated or upset because of someone else's opinions. If someone has a way of speaking you find strange don't focus on their delivery instead focus on the message their trying to get across.

8. Tone - Strong speakers will use tone and volume to get across their message. Let the way their saying something help you in understanding the message their trying to deliver.

9. Listen For The Ideas - When listening you want to link together the information a speaker is giving you and figure out the overall message.

10. Watch For Non Verbal Cues - We also listen with our eyes. We can often learn a lot of additional information just through the different facial expressions and mannerisms the speaker is giving off.

2. Clarification / Reflection Skills

These are two common skills that one uses to ensure that the things they've heard and interpreted is the intended message.

No matter how good you believe your at skills at listening are, the one person who can let you know if you're understanding the information correctly is the speaker themselves. So as an extension of your listening skills, you'll want to develop the skill of reflecting feelings and words to help clarify that you're understanding them properly.

Reflection

Reflecting is a process that involves restating and paraphrasing the words and feelings of the person speaking. The purpose of reflection is to let the speaker hear their thoughts out loud, focusing on what their saying and feeling. It's also used to show your speaker that you're trying to empathize with them and view things from their viewpoint. Reflection also encourage the speaker to continue the dialogue and sharing information.

When reflecting you're not introducing new topics, asking questions, or moving the conversation in a new direction. Reflection allows a speaker to feel understood, and it also gives them a chance to refocus their ideas. This can lead to them further discussing their thoughts and clarifying what their trying to get across.

<u>There's two main techniques used in reflection;</u>

1. Paraphrasing - This technique involves using other words to help reflect back what the speaker previously said. This technique shows you're actively listening and attempting to better understand what the speaker has to say. People often hear what they want to hear. Their listening is clouded by their own prejudices and assumptions. When you paraphrase it's important not to inject your point of view or feelings. You want to remain non judgmental. This skill can take some time to get comfortable using and is even tricky for more emotionally intelligent people. Give it time you'll get the hang of it.

2. Mirroring - This is the simpler of the two techniques. It involves saying back what the speaker said almost word for word. This should only be used for simple and short ideas or thoughts. When mirroring back to the speaker it's okay to repeat only a few of the key words and last words they spoke. It lets the speaker know you've been listening and are attempting to understand them. Don't overuse this technique. It can quickly become irritating and distracting. People can mirror back both words and body language.

Clarification

Clarification is a process that involves checking that the listener is correct in their understanding of the speaker's message, resolving any areas of misunderstanding or confusion. Clarification is very important because communication can often be difficult, with emotional or complex messages being discussed. You want to make sure you understand otherwise you could interpret things incorrectly and assume things that shouldn't be assumed.

Clarifying a speaker's statements reassures them that you're listening and trying to understand what they're expressing. To clarify you can ask open and closed non judgmental questions, along with occasionally summarizing what they were saying in a better attempt to understand it.

Some open questions you might ask to help assist the person speaking to expand upon their thoughts include:

What made you feel this particular way?

At what point did you begin feeling like this?

Some closed questions you might ask to get a simple yes or no answer from your speaker include:

Have you always felt like this?

Were you aware that you felt this way?

Guidelines on Clarification

Use these guidelines to aid you in understanding and better communicating with the other speaker.

If you're unsure what the speaker meant by something let them know it.

Don't be afraid to ask the speaker to repeat what they said.

Ask the speaker for examples.

Summarize what the speaker said, and ask if this is what they were really saying.

Ask the speaker if you understood the message and be open to getting corrected by them.

If you follow all these steps and guidelines you'll have mastered both the art of reflection and clarification in no time. Don't be afraid or nervous to ask for clarification. Avoiding this will lead to poor communication and bigger issues down the road.

Conflict Management

Conflict and disputes are a part of life. In this section, I'm going to discuss conflict as it relates to our social interactions. Conflict often arises when people start to feel added stress, anger of a situation they deem unfair, or from the loss of something or someone important. Learning how to manage these situations easily and effectively requires a higher level of emotional intelligence.

Unresolved conflict has been shown to lead to serious health issues as the added stress damages your body, leading to higher blood pressure and even heart attacks. That's why learning to deal with our conflict in a constructive and positive manner is important. It will not only improve your health but it will improve your relationships in the long run.

So first off, what is conflict? Well, interpersonal conflict is often defined as:

"A struggle between at least two different parties who both feel they have incompatible goals and feel there is interference from the other side in the achievement of their goals".

There are generally three types of different conflicts:

1. *Personal / Relational Conflict* - This type of conflict usually revolves around self image, identity, or another important aspect of relationships like perceived betrayal, disloyalty, and disrespect.

2. *Instrumental Conflict* - This type of conflict is related to procedures and goals. This can relate to both personal and professional situations.

3. *Conflict of Interest* - This type of conflict is related to things like space, knowledge, time, and money. It deals with how those things are allotted when we've achieved our goal. One example, would be a husband and wife disagreeing over whether to spend a Christmas bonus on an upgrade to the house or a family vacation.

In general, it's easier to deal with conflict the sooner you can no matter what type of conflict it is. Over time people become more entrenched in their positions. If you catch things early, friends and family are less likely to already have taken a side, and any negative emotions haven't had a chance to build and get too extreme.

Five strategies for dealing with conflict:

1. _Compete / Fight_ - In this situation, the person who has more power in the relationship will usually win the conflict. Not a good option as it creates a loser. This will only lead to bad feelings down the road. You want conflicts to be resolved in a win win situation whenever possible.

2. _Collaboration_ - An ideal situation where both parties work through their issues and find a way to work together in order to find a solution so that all parties come out happy. This can be a difficult one to achieve and can require a good amount of time when both parties are entrenched in their position.

3. _Avoidance / Denial_ - This might be good as a way to cool down from a conflict. Something to use before an eventual discussion takes place or if the conflict is minor enough that avoiding it won't lead to issues down the road. I suggest only using this to gain your composure before dealing with the conflict in a more productive fashion. This type of strategy can be lose / lose as bad feelings will still be lingering on both sides.

4. _Negotiation / Compromise_ - This is where both set of parties are willing to give up something and essentially meet in the middle. This is my second favorite tactic. It's easier to pull off than collaboration, but it also requires less commitment in achieving the outcome and therefore can be less successful.

5. _Smoothing Over_ - This is where harmony and peace are maintained on the surface, however, underneath there is still conflict. This can work in preserving relationships but is usually a win / lose scenario where one person is still not alright with things being smoothed over.

When dealing with conflicts you need to be assertive and willing to actively listen to each side. Everyone is entitled to their point of view and just because you're not in agreement doesn't automatically mean you're right. Learn to empathize with the other side and see things from their position. I suggest always trying to collaborate or at least compromise. The other strategies are often only temporary band aids.

Conflict isn't always a bad thing. While it can be destructive and a waste of time that causes hard feelings, it can also help to clear the air of grievances, and lead to a constructive resolution that improves long term relationships and releases pent up emotions, tension, and stress. If you go into each conflict with a positive mindset and armed with your communication skills you'll find that you're often able to reach a happier outcome.

Chapter Five : 100+ Skills, Tips & Tricks to Improve Your Emotional Intelligence & Mindfulness

6 Emotional Intelligence Skills

In this section, I'm going to discuss a few emotional intelligence skills you'll want to begin mastering. These skills will benefit you long term in every area of your life. There's no downside by improving on these skills. It will make you a more well rounded person capable of things you may have not previously thought possible.

1. *Empathy* - High EQ people are usually skilled at being able to put themselves in the shoes of those around them. This is an excellent skill to focus on as the insight you'll gain from being more empathetic will allow you to connect with others and teach you things about yourself you hadn't yet learned.

2. *Active Listening* - By listening before reacting you give yourself the space to take all your own feelings and thoughts into account. Listening also helps to drain the tension out of certain situations by letting the talker get their feelings off their chest. If you're defensive and react without listening you'll often only further the conflict.

3. *Mindful Breathing* - People experience their emotions physically. This means when we get stressed our bodies will react as if we're being threatened or attacked. It's part our very nature to do this. However, if we're able to calm our reaction to this stress, the body won't be taxed nearly as hard. One of the key ways to do this is by practicing mindful breathing. Whenever you start feeling tense, begin breathing in deeply and slowly, concentrating only on the breath, letting it flow in and out of your body. After a couple of minutes you'll begin noticing a difference. This is because your body is now in a more relaxed state. Practicing this will allow you to keep your emotions under control and allow you to make more informed decisions.

4. *Apply Consequential Thinking* - For instance, when somethings gets you mad or upset take a deep breath and then think through the action you're going to take assessing any benefits and costs it may have. This will train you to be more careful when making choices in the future.

5. *Acknowledgment* - Being able to acknowledge feelings that are both positive and negative will allow you to gain valuable information about yourself and make you more self aware.

6. *Reading Body Language* - Practice reading the body language and facial expressions of people as there having conversations. Look for how they physically react with each emotion. Personally, I read a book on body language and practiced studying it a few minutes each day when an opportunity presented itself. At first I wasn't great at picking up the different cues but over the course of a few months I got really good at knowing how people felt just by how they were carrying themselves. It's a great skill to learn. I've found it to be invaluable in both personal and professional settings.

96 *Emotional Intelligence Tips & Tricks*

1. Be open to criticism and feedback. Be receptive to learning how other people view you and use that information to make any necessary adjustments.

2. Take the time to sponsor and mentor employees that have earned it.

3. Make an extra effort to be polite and thank people. When people are at ease around you they will be willing to perform harder for you.

4. Identify how you feel at multiple times of the day. Make a mental note when something triggers a strong reaction from you. You can use this information to learn what things you need to work on.

5. Employees appreciate management that are willing to share their privileges and perks.

6. Be consistent with your behavior and how you treat others.

7. Show that you're a thoughtful person. People respond to this much more than you might think. It will make achieving your objectives and goals much easier.

8. I suggest practicing mindfulness in all facets of your every day life. Being mindful of everything around you allows you to become extremely aware of your own feelings and the feelings of others.

9. Take the time to celebrate any positive emotions. You'll find if you take the time to recognize your positive emotions they'll begin to occur more frequently. This will allow you to have better personal and professional relationships.

10. Show that you care about people. This gesture is more powerful than you might think in enabling you to achieve your leadership goals and objectives.

11. Before you act. Take a moment to pause, acknowledge any feelings or thoughts, and then clear your mind.

12. Take one long deep breath before you respond to something or someone when you're emotionally fired up. This pause will allow you the time needed to gather yourself.

13. Try and be compassionate in everything you do. While you won't always be successful coming at things from this angle will make you more in tune with the feelings of those around you.

14. If you hit some type of set back, take a moment to step back and analyze what you can and cannot control in the situation. If you can't control something let go of it and move on. This will allow you to focus on the things you can control in order to move past the set back.

15. A good practice technique to use is when you have an issue take a moment to consider it and then write down two solutions to it. This will get your mind used to thinking about problems before instinctively reacting to them.

16. Take stock of your strengths and than try to use them more often to your advantage.

17. Take stock of your weaknesses and find a way to gradually improve on them.

18. Learn to sense your emotions in advance so you won't get surprised or overwhelmed by them.

19. Once you've learned to acknowledge your different emotions stop to ask yourself what can be done about them and come up with solutions.

20. Try and stop your low EQ habits. These include judging other people critically. This is a difficult one for most people. Another one is taking offense when people are critical of you. It's easy to get defensive but it's not beneficial. You should be learning how to rid yourself of the bad habits replacing them with habits that will benefit you mentally and spiritually.

21. When at work have a feelings board available for your employees. This can be a white board simply split into three parts of the days with a list of emotions. Have your employees mark how they felt during each part of the day and then assess how your staff was feeling and when they felt certain things. You can begin to observe patterns by doing this and create solutions to help ease any negative low points that may arise for a majority of the staff during certain parts of the day.

22. Remember your emotions aren't just feelings. Try and understand what the message is behind your emotions. This will allow you a greater understanding of yourself.

23. Create a positive environment around you. Start cutting out the influences that are negatively influencing you and replace them with ones that benefit you. Having a positive environment will allow you to open up and grow as a person.

24. Model your behavior after other high EQ people. No need to blaze a new trail when a perfectly good one has already been created to show you the way.

25. Embrace new ideas, people, and experiences. These will all teach you and offer opportunities for positive growth. Use them to your benefit.

26. Look for the best in others and don't ever be ashamed to ask for help. People with high levels of emotional intelligence realize their personal limitations and are open to support and help from the people around them.

27. Don't fear change. It's a natural part of life. Emotionally intelligent people accept that the world will throw a curve ball from time to time. Having the ability to adapt means you can roll with the punches and look at change as a new opportunity instead of as something to be upset about.

28. Don't withhold intimacy from your loved ones. The more emotionally intelligent you are the more open you are to sharing your whole self with those around you. Don't hold back out of fear. Instead let the people you care about know the real you.

29. Be intellectually curious. Growth is life. Always be exploring and learning new things about the world and people around you. If you don't seek out knowledge you'll never be able to evolve as a person.

30. Put yourself in other people's shoes. Your viewpoint isn't the only one or even always the right one. Allow yourself a few moments to look at things in a new perspective. Doing so will allow you to come into any discussion with an open mind free of judgment.

31. Take responsibility for your own actions and feelings. If you do or feel something your not proud of own up to it and try to do better next time. No one is perfect, everyone will stumble and fall along the way. Don't get down on yourself, instead look at it as an opportunity to learn something new about yourself.

32. Don't hold things in. Doing this isn't healthy and will cause you to eventually lose control of your emotions and blow up. Work through your issues as they come up.

33. Don't let other people dictate how you feel about yourself. You need to be confident in yourself and your abilities. Don't let other people's opinions determine your self worth.

34. Practice conveying what you're thinking in a non threatening manner. Be respectful of those around you.

35. Emotionally intelligent people aren't afraid to share the way they feel. Practice sharing whenever possible.

36. Check your ego. Be open to other people's viewpoints and opinions. Don't let your ego get in the way of connecting with others.

37. Don't give guilt trips to the people around you. If you have an issue deal with it head on. Don't dance around the problem. Be direct but not rude or inconsiderate. Let the people in your life know where they stand with you. Don't do things like slam the door or give an attitude.

38. Emotionally intelligent people don't believe in manipulating others or resorting to mind games. Don't prey on the weakness or kindness of others. Treat people like you'd expect them to treat you.

39. You don't need to win your conversation or argument. It's not a competition. Be open to hearing their side and consider what they have to say. Don't invalidate what they're telling you because you aren't in agreement with them.

40. Don't hold your intellect over the people around you. If you're smarter or more informed on an issue don't lord the fact over those around you. Instead be humble and if someone wants more information share it with them without being condescending.

41. High EQ people are normally very well balanced individuals. They don't tend to be too optimistic or too pessimistic. Work on finding ways to keep an even keel even when faced with stressful or unpleasant situations.

42. Emotionally intelligent people aren't bogged down with things like fear, shame, guilt, obligation, and embarrassment. Work on facing the negative emotions and feeling comfortable in your own skin.

43. Work on becoming more present in your daily life. You can't control the past or the future. There's no reason to continue living anywhere but in the here and now.

44. Don't shut out the people in your life. Many low EQ people will seek a substitute relationship that they are able to control. This can be with other people, getting additional pets, or even creating fictional relationships. Deal with the issue, don't replace it with something else hoping your problems will disappear.

45. Learn to recognize your feelings. Feelings about something don't mean that something is a fact. Just because your heart says one thing doesn't mean it's true. High EQ people are able to separate their feelings from the reality of situation.

46. Give yourself the gift of meditation and silence. Allow yourself time to just be in the moment. I suggest doing this on a daily basis if possible.

47. Learn the benefit of denying yourself immediate satisfaction for long term gain. This can be either at work or at home. Don't sacrifice future goals, success and happiness just because a lesser option can be achieved now. Learn the value of saying no and waiting for what you really desire.

48. Learn to trust in your decisions. The more confident you become in your decision making process the more you'll be able to trust your intuition is guiding you the right way. High EQ people know when to trust themselves.

49. Practice humility. High EQ people don't see the need to brag or boast about who they are or what they are able to do.

50. Practice talking with new people in public settings. The more comfortable you get connecting with strangers, the more you'll begin to pick up on people's verbal and non verbal cues going forward.

51. Emotionally intelligent people are often happier people. They are better able to control their moods and on a whole suffer fewer mood swings or exhibit signs of depression. Work towards controlling the way you feel. The more you practice finding ways to feel happy the easier it will become over time.

52. Learn to give expecting not to receive anything else in return. Being able to give a piece of yourself unselfishly shows a high level of emotional intelligence.

53. Don't take yourself that seriously. Learn to ease up and laugh at yourself sometimes. It's hard to connect with someone always uptight and self serious.

54. High EQ people realize there's no such things as perfection. Knowing this means they are able to forgive themselves and others for mistakes and other foibles.

55. Learn to take breaks and disconnect. Emotionally intelligent people realize there needs to be times when you recharge and rest. Being able to take care of your basic needs is more important than work.

56. Realize you're in charge of your own life. High EQ people understand that it's up to them to take care of both their mental and physical well being. You are the one who ultimately knows what things you need out of life.

57. Avoid any toxic people in your life. Don't let yourself be dragged down by these type of people. These people will only add frustration and unnecessary problems to your life.

58. Don't sit on the fence about issues. Be committed to your view on things. If you believe in something follow it.

59. Don't edit or judge your feelings too fast. Take the time to understand what you're feeling and why you feel it.

60. See if you're able to make any type of connection between how you feel and when you feel it. Doing this will allow you to find certain situations or times that bring up certain feelings. This will allow you to find ways to resolve your issues or understand them better.

61. If you're not sure how you feel ask someone else what they think you're feeling by your current demeanor. Often others can sense how we're feeling by our current actions and moods. This will allow you to also see how other people view you and help you align those views with your personal view of yourself.

62. Keep a log book of how you feel, Everyday rate how you're feeling on a scale of 1 through 100 and what you were currently doing. I like to do this three times a day and then go over the results each week to see if I notice any patterns good or bad.

63. Keep a journal about your feelings and what caused them. Doing this often will teach you to diagnose how your feeling at any current moment. I've found this one to be very helpful in raising my EQ.

64. Use a dream journal. Dreams can often tell us how we're really feeling. Keeping a journal of these dreams will let us figure out and analyze those feelings easier.

65. Try some free association to get more in tune with how your feeling unconsciously.

66. Name your emotions. During the day when something causes you to have an emotion try saying the emotion out loud. It sounds silly but when you get in the habit of naming your emotions you'll quickly begin to raise your EQ by learning to better recognize how your feeling.

67. Recognize how certain emotions make your body feel. Does happiness make you feel a sense of warmth? Does stress give you knots in your muscles and stomach?

68. Learn to recognize how your emotions connect to your actions each day. If you're embarrassed do you shy away from conversation? If you're angry do you lash out at others?

69. Begin to look for patterns in the emotions your feeling. Knowing the "why" of things will help you increase positive emotion and decrease negative ones.

70. Remember that you decide on the way you're going to behave. Your behavior is a choice. You can choose to be open and compassionate or an obnoxious jerk.

71. Keep an open mind. Studies have shown people with narrow views have lower EQ than those who are open to new ideas and ways of thinking.

72. When you see someone else have a strong emotional reaction to something ask yourself how would you react if the same scenario were to happen to you.

73. Stay engaged while conversing with others. Don't let your mind drift off. Be in the moment. Ask questions and really make an effort to understand the person you're talking to.

74. Learn to read body language. If this doesn't come naturally to you. Read up on body language to learn the different emotional tells and then begin to watch your friends to see if you can discern how they feel strictly through physical non verbal cues.

75. Learn the effect you have on those around you. How do you make people feel with your presence. Are people comfortable around you? Are they looking for the exit? Maybe they are nervous or intimidated? EQ is as much inward as it is outward. You want people to feel drawn and connected to you.

76. High EQ people thrive in jobs that have a lot of social interaction. Consider this when looking at career opportunities.

77. Work on discovering your inner passions. Find what gives your life meaning. This will naturally make you motivated and happier. Having a sense of purpose is a great stress reducer.

78. Be more socially responsible. Try giving either your time or money to a charity you care about. Work on projects that will help to improve your community or the lives of those who matter to you.

79. Practice managing your impulses. You can use different tricks to help you get good at not giving into impulse. Some things to try include distracting yourself or stopping and analyzing the reason behind the impulse.

80. Be flexible. You need to be open to change. Being too rigid will stifle opportunity and progress. High EQ people know when to make adjustments and when to let go of things that are holding them back. Don't become too emotionally attached to one way of doing things or a certain set of routines.

81. Practice listening. Listening is an art form unto itself. Learn to read between the lines to really understand what the people around you are trying to convey.

82. Appreciate what you have in life. Learning to appreciate things allows you to be a happier more well balanced person. You can strive for more and appreciate what you have at the same time.

83. Teach your children the value of emotional intelligence at a young age. Give them tasks and exercises to get them in touch with their feelings and the feelings of those around them.

84. Use gentle humor to express things that might otherwise be hard to discuss.

85. Be playful. Being silly and playful will ease the tension in a room and allow others around you to relax and feel at ease.

86. Use your non verbal cues. You can guide conversations with things like the tone of your voice, eye contact, and body position. If done right it will allow you to resolve conflict and tension in stressful situations.

87. Take responsibility. If you're at fault own up to that fact to the people around you. This will make those around you respect you more for how you hold yourself.

88. When you hurt someone apologize right away. Don't let negative feelings linger. Resolve conflict as quickly as possibly.

89. Try and notice if the people that you're most connected with behave like you. Start to realize if someone is just trying to tell you what you want to hear or they're genuine in their communication with you.

90. Learn to gauge people's readiness for change. Change doesn't come overnight. Most people will deny that a change will need to be made before accepting it and trying to work on themselves. Learning to do this shows you've gotten a deeper understanding of the people around you.

91. Always set clear goals for your employees. Let them know what's expected of them and when. Being able to do this effectively shows you have good leadership skills.

92. When training employees don't be afraid to try experimental methods. Working in groups, role playing, and simulations are better ways to engage your employees and train them to be more interconnected with the people around around them and your customers. It will help to improve their EQ level.

93. Learn to prepare your employees for failure. Let them know that slip ups will occur and show them how to rebound without letting things spiral downward. Learning to help others set realistic expectations shows a high level of emotional intelligence.

94. Support learning and foster a culture of creativity in the workplace. It will teach your employees to seek out new ways to find answers and make them more adaptable.

95. Practice putting your strengths and skills into everyday use. Determine what you're good at and find ways to use those things to your benefit. Playing to your strengths will allow you to achieve more at a faster rate.

96. Understand that emotional intelligence is a process that will evolve over the course of your lifetime. This isn't something you can learn and master over a weekend. Practice these skills and steps and you'll naturally become more emotionally intelligent over time.

58 Mindfulness Tips for Beginner's

In this section I'll go over 55+ tips that will help you become more mindful over yourself and your surroundings. I have this list in a file on my computer that I can reference whenever I feel the need to refocus. I hope these tips have the same positive impact on your life that they did in mine.

1. Whenever you need to relax, simply concentrate only on your breathing and allow your subconscious to take over.

2. When driving, turn off all music or talk radio, experiencing the sound of silence. It takes a bit to get used to. You'll feel like something may be missing. However, after time you'll see that with silence you're able to otherwise fill your mind with different perceptions, many of which are very rewarding. Practicing this can leave your mind calmer, quieter and much more focused overall.

3. Eat slower than normal. Try eating a meal in silence each week as an experiment. This will help you experience the eating more fully. You may also want to cut out reading, listening to music, or watching TV while you're eating. Eliminating these things will allow you to become more attuned with how you eat and will give you more awareness when you're eating among other people.

4. When you're working, use your breaks to really relax instead of just pausing on what you're doing. For example, instead of having a drink and talking with your fellow workers, take a short walk and meditate.

5. Be aware of how often you're letting your mind dwell on past memories or future possibilities. Is this something that is necessary? Are these memories affecting you negatively? The future and the past are places we visit for planning and learning. However, many of us end up living in the past or future, instead of focusing on the here and now. Don't let yourself fall into that trap.

6. Use your environmental cues as a reminder to continually center yourself. Allow the cues around you to help signal to yourself that it's time you take a minute to pause, take a deep breath, and become more aware of your bodily sensation. When you do this it allows your mind to settle down and regroup.

7. When going to work and stopped at a light, take a moment to pay close attention to what's around you, where your mind is at, and your breathing.

8. When your done with your work day and you're walking to your vehicle, focus on your breathing and the air around you. Listen to any sounds you hear. Your goal is to be able to walk without the feeling of being rushed. You shouldn't feel anxious to get home.

9. When you get home after work, be sure to say hello to everyone in your home. Look into each of their eyes when doing this. Afterward, take about 5-15 minutes to stay quiet and still. If you happen to live by yourself, enter your home and embrace the quietness of your environment and the feeling of that silence.

10. Spend some more time in nature. I take long walks and hikes whenever possible.

11. Notice how your mind is constantly judging things. Don't take these judgments too seriously. These thoughts aren't who you are.

12. Practice listening without judging. It's harder to do than it sounds.

13. Don't feel forced to always be doing something. If you have some free time take that time to simply be.

14. When walking, be aware of how your weight is shifting, the sensations you feel in your feet. Focus more on yourself and less on where you're headed.

15. Take some time to focus only on your breathing. Feel the flow of your breath and how your chest rises and falls.

16. Take notice of what you're doing while you're doing it. Try and be in tune with all your senses.

17. When you're eating, notice the texture and colors of your food as well as how it tastes.

18. If your mind begins to wander to negative thinking, bring it back gently to your breath.

19. Remember your thoughts are only thoughts, You aren't obligated to react to them or even believe them.

20. Think of all the activities you do that you tend to zone out in. Some examples are texting, doing chores, web surfing, & driving. Take some time and practice being more aware when participating in these activities.

21. Practice short bursts of mindfulness. Our brains react better to shorter sessions of mindfulness many times throughout the day, rather than a few long sessions of being mindful.

22. Pick out a prompt to help you remember to be mindful. It could be getting a cup of coffee triggers you to take some time to be mindful, or hanging your coat up when you get home from work. Whatever triggers help you remember to practice mindfulness on daily basis will work just fine.

23. Learn to properly meditate. Mindfulness is a skill we need to learn and sharpen over time. Being able to meditate properly will allow you to accomplish this.

24. Practice being mindful while you're waiting. Whether it's in line or at a doctor's appointment, these moments are great opportunities to practice being more mindful.

25. Practice first thing when you wake up in the morning. I find this helps me set the tone for the rest of my day and gets my body more in tune with my surroundings. Take a few minutes before you start reading your paper, watching TV, or getting ready for whatever tasks you have on hand that day.

26. Right after waking up, before getting out of your bed, focus on your breathing. Observe at least 5 mindful breaths.

27. Be aware of changes in posture. You need to stay aware of how your mind and body feel when you're going from lying down, up to sitting, up to standing, up to walking. Notice your posture from one transition to the next.

28. Use any sound you hear as a bell for mindfulness. Really use that opportunity to listen and be present.

29. During the course of your day, take a moment from time to time to focus on your breathing. Observe 5 mindful breaths.

30. Pay attention when you're eating. Consciously consume your food, bringing awareness to tasting, chewing, and swallowing. Realize that your food was connected to something that helped nourish its growth.

31. Bring awareness to talking and listening. Can you listen to someone without either agreeing or disagreeing, disliking or liking, or planning what things you'll say when it's your turn to talk? While talking, can you simply state what you need to say without understating or overstating? Are you able to notice how both your body and mind feel? The more you practice being aware and present the easier it'll get over time.

32. Focus some more attention on your normal everyday activities. These include washing, brushing your teeth, and getting dressed. Try and practice bringing mindfulness to each of these activities.

33. Notice any points on your body where you're feeling tight. Try and breathe into them, while exhaling let go of any excess tension you feel. Do you have tension stored in any part of your body. For example, your shoulders, neck, jaw, stomach or back? If so, try stretching and practicing yoga at least once each day.

34. Before bed, take a moment to bring some attention to your breathing. The same as you did when you wake up in the morning. Observe 5 mindful breaths.

35. Create a 15 minute invite on your calendar regarding mindfulness for each day and be sure to commit to always spending that time with yourself.

36. Take breaks from your job to help gain perspective on what you're doing.

37. Find some other people at your job who are interested in becoming more mindful and practice your mindfulness together.

38. Find a mindfulness mentor. This can be anyone practicing that you can get advice from and can talk about your practicing with.

39. Focus on individual tasks instead of trying to multitask.

40. Try and take a walk outside every day leaving your phone behind or turned off.

41. Try riding a bike to work. You'll need to be mindful if you're biking through some traffic.

42. Pause and center yourself for about 30 seconds at your job before diving into the work you have to accomplish.

43. Turn a unused closet or room into a meditation space.

44. Implement boundaries to help let your mind shut off. For instance turn off your phone after 9 pm or don't bring it in your bedroom before going to sleep.

45. Don't beat yourself up if you get distracted. There will be days that are far more hectic than others.

46. They call it "practice" for a good reason – It takes a lot of repetition to properly develop your mindfulness muscle.

47. Not everyone will develop there mindfulness habits at the same pace. For some it may take as little as 8 weeks. For others it will take longer. Just keep going and you'll get there eventually.

48. Don't get dragged down by your problems. Problems can be an opportunity to grow. Learn to recognize problems and solve them.

49. Don't wallow in your past. Live each day without regret. The more you look to the past the harder it will be to enjoy your time in the present.

50. Always create new goals for yourself. Give yourself something to look forward to each day.

51. Take time to appreciate yourself. If you can't learn to find value in yourself you'll have a hard time finding it in others.

52. Learn something new everyday. Even if it's something small. Continued growth and knowledge will only benefit you in the long run. Making mistakes is par for the course. It's only that we learn from our mistakes that matters.

53. Appreciate the small things your friends and family do for you. Do small things for the people in your life to show how much you care.

54. Mindfulness is not something to do a few minutes a day. Over time it should become a part of your life. The goal is to bring more awareness and compassion to every situation you find yourself in. Learning how to be more mindful in all situations will only benefit you long term.

55. Try out aromatherapy to increase your focus. I've found that smell helps me focus more than chants or mantras. Most people don't think to try aromatherapy. I know I didn't at first.

56. Have an open and clean space to meditate in. You want as little distraction surrounding you as possible when meditating. This especially rings true when you're first starting out. Try to find an area that is free of clutter and distraction when meditating at home.

57. Let in some air and natural light to your meditation area. Many people, myself included, are able to focus much better when breathing in fresh air and surrounded by sunlight.

58. Choose the kind of meditation that resonates with you. Don't practice a form of meditation just because it's what someone said you should do. Learn the different methods, and decide for yourself. The more comfortable you are, the better chance you'll have at sticking with it. While I enjoy mindfulness meditation and walking meditations, my partner prefers yoga and guided sitting meditations.

Chapter Six: A Guide to Emotional Intelligence Apps, Tests, Books, & Resources

Emotional Intelligence Resources

In this section I'll discuss and share with you three different emotional intelligence resources you can use to help aid you in your quest of becoming more emotionally intelligent. I've learned things from all of these sites and recommend you check them out to see if they can be of help to you as well.

1. 6 Seconds - Amazing EQ site filled with loads of information, profiles, events, certification courses and other resources. My favorite site on the subject. Has some excellent books, games and curriculum you can purchase off their site to help you improve your EQ level.

2. Emotional Intelligence Consortium - Great reference site. Lots of articles and information.

3. EQ - A free online community dedicated to teaching people about emotional intelligence and how it affects each area of our lives.

Emotional Intelligence Apps

In this section I'll discuss and share with you seven different emotional intelligence apps you can use in your daily life. Not all of these apps will apply to everyone. Please feel free to pick the ones that best work for you. Many of these have made an impact in my EQ growth. I highly recommend them.

1. Intend - This app is available for free on IOS. Focus your intentions, raise your level of awareness and change how you behave. Found this app to be quite helpful.

2. Emotion Wheel - This app is available for free on IOS. Track all your emotions and use it to help you become more self aware.

3. EQ Coach - This app is available for free on IOS and also has a paid full version for $1.99. Offers a powerful set of questions to help you become better at self reflection and raise your EQ level. This one benefited me when I was first starting out.

4. Mood Meter - Available on both Android and IOS. Costs $0.99 on both platforms. Let's you check in with how your feeling and helps to build your level of emotional intelligence over time. Based on years of research done at the highly esteemed Yale University.

5. Stop, Breathe, & Think - This app is available for free on Android, IOS, and the Web. Has a good mix of basic meditations that range in length. This app is great for helping you become more mindful and self aware.

6. IF... The Emotional IQ Game - This app is available on the IOS. It's free to try and has in app purchases. Great game for kids to help teach them emotional and social skills.

7. Omvana - This app is available on Android, IOS, and the Web. Offers over 500 of the top audios on meditation, mind, body, lifestyle, productivity and relationships. It comes with guided meditations from famous authors and a variety of inspirational tracks to help you get inspired each day. This app is free to download and then has in app purchases ranging from .99 cents to $7.99. This is an app worth checking out and offers a ton of content.

Emotional Intelligence Tests

Here are a handful of tests and quizzes you can take to gauge your level of emotional intelligence in a variety of areas. Gives you a good way to determine where you're starting out and how far you need to go.

1. Emotional Intelligence Test - Free test to gauge your level of emotional intelligence.

http://www.ihhp.com/free-eq-quiz/

2. Emotionally Intelligent Leadership Quiz - Quick quiz to determine your leadership ability.

http://www.workingresources.com/eileadershipsurvey/emoti onally-intelligent-leadership-quiz.html

3. Interview / Selecting Emotionally Intelligent People Quiz - Quick quiz to help you see how good your at selecting emotionally intelligent people for your workplace.

http://www.workingresources.com/selectingemotionallyintelli gentpeople/selecting-emotionally-intelligent-people-quiz.html

4. MEIT Test - Free test of 40 questions testing your level of emotional intelligence.

http://www.maetrix.com.au/meit/eitest.html

5. Goleman's EQ Test - Free basic EQ test from acclaimed author Daniel Goleman.

http://www.arealme.com/eq/en/

Emotional Intelligence Books

Here's are my two favorite EQ books. I learned a lot from each of these and definitely recommend them for a more in depth look at emotional intelligence, the role it plays in our life, and how can improve our own levels of EQ.

1. Emotional Intelligence by Daniel Goleman - The acclaimed #1 bestselling book. An in depth look at emotional intelligence by one of the leader's in the field.

2. Emotional Intelligence 2.0 by Travis Bradberry & Jean Greaves - Another great book on EQ that focuses on teaching step by step how to improve your emotional intelligence level.

Body Language Books

Here's are my two favorite books on body language. I learned a ton from each of these and highly recommend them for learning how to properly read the people around you. It will not only allow you to connect with them easier but it will teach you a lot about your own body language and the messages you give off to other people.

1. The Definitive Book of Body Language by Barbara & Allan Pease - The #1 international bestselling guide to body language. This is my personal favorite.

2. What Every Body Is Saying by Joe Navarro & Marvin Karlins - This one is by an ex FBI agent who spent years reading people teaches you how to speed read the people around and determine what their non verbal cues are telling you about themselves.

Conclusion

Thanks again for purchasing my book. Being emotionally intelligent is something to strive for. It means working towards becoming the very best version of yourself. While this work can be difficult and frustrating at times it's well worth the effort. The more open you are and the more you're able to communicate with the people around you, the richer your life will be both privately and professionally.

Personally, I've found that working on my own emotional intelligence has done wonders for my life. It's made me a more caring and compassionate friend, business operator, and partner. I've learned that I feel better when I'm in control of my emotions. I no longer get worked up about the little things that used to drive me crazy. Gone is the added stress brought on by anger. I found that practicing the skills I went over in this book along with some of the different mindfulness techniques I've learned over the years has transformed me from the person I was just a few short years ago. Not only has my personal relationships gotten better but my business has grown and opportunities have come my way that I never thought were once possible.

I hope you realize the many benefits of improving your emotional intelligence level after reading this book.

Good luck! I wish you nothing but the best!

66183027R00042

Made in the USA
Lexington, KY
05 August 2017